Beginner's Guide to
Beadwork

*To Daniel, Paige
and all my family*

Beginner's Guide to
Beadwork

Madeleine Rollason

SEARCH PRESS

First published in Great Britain 2004

Search Press Limited
Wellwood, North Farm Road,
Tunbridge Wells, Kent TN2 3DR

Reprinted 2004

Text and beaded designs copyright
© Madeleine Rollason 2004

Photographs by Charlotte de la Bédoyère and Steve Crispe,
Search Press Studios

Photographs and design copyright
© Search Press Ltd. 2004

ISBN 1903975 39 5

The Publishers and author can accept no responsibility for
any consequences arising from the information, advice or
instructions given in this publication.

Readers are permitted to reproduce any of the items in
this book for their personal use, or for the purposes of
selling for charity, free of charge and without the prior
permission of the Publishers. Any use of the items for
commercial purposes is not permitted without the prior
permission of the Publishers.

Suppliers

If you have difficulty in obtaining any of the materials and
equipment mentioned in this book, then please visit the
Search Press website for details of suppliers:
www.searchpress.com

Alternatively, you can write to the Publishers at the
address above, for a current list of stockists, including
firms who operate a mail-order service.

Publishers' note

All the step-by-step photographs in this book feature
the author, Madeleine Rollason, demonstrating her
beadwork techniques. No models have been used.

Acknowledgements

I would like to thank:

*my family, especially my husband, Ian, for their
patience and tolerance at having our home
turned into a bead sanctuary;*

*Gemma Cartwright, for her encouragement
and support in writing this book;*

*Anne Wallace, for testing my patterns and
offering her expertise and keen insights;*

*Minnie Murray, for testing my patterns and
sharing her wealth of experience;*

*and Rachel Saward from Search Press for
modelling some of the finished pieces.*

Page 1
Amethyst bracelet
See also page 57.

Page 3
Queen for a day
Beaded bead in peyote and brick stitch.

Page 2
Beaded bone egg
*Believed to date from the 1850s. British.
The hollow egg is in two parts and holds a miniature
set of dominoes.*

Page 5
Curiosity pot
*This little pot, measuring 6.4 x 2.8cm (2½ x 1½in), is
worked in herringbone stitch.*

Printed in Malaysia by Times Offset (M) Sdn Bhd

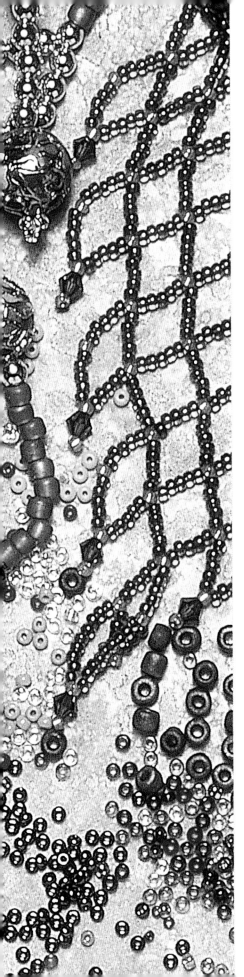

Contents

Introduction

My love of beads is such that I am often called a *beadaholic*. I have always been involved with crafts of one sort or another – knitting, crochet, embroidery, tapestry, etc. – and enjoyed them all. But, when I bought my first beading kit I was hooked, and spent all my free time trying different techniques. Beads are beautiful and versatile and there is an enormous range of colours, sizes and finishes to choose from. With beads it is possible to make jewellery, small pots, three-dimensional sculptures, wall hangings and you can even decorate clothes and furnishings; the list is endless.

Some time later I started my own beading business and this gave me the opportunity to spend all day working with beads. I jumped at the chance of writing this book as it meant that I could write about what I love most (apart from my husband and family of course!).

I hope that, as you read through this book, you too will come to appreciate the art and craft of beading. But, be warned – beads are addictive! Sometimes, I wake up in the early hours of the morning with an idea I must try out, or cannot get to sleep because my mind is wondering how a picture or object would look when worked up in beads. There is a saying in my house, 'if it sits still long enough, Madeleine will bead it!'

This is a beginner's guide and, as such, I have focused on basic off-loom beading techniques. However, my hope is that the detailed step-by-step demonstrations will encourage you to experiment and give you the confidence to develop your beading skills.

History

Although there does not seem to be an official history of beads, they are known to have been used as adornment and status symbols for thousands of years around the world. Very early beads were hand made from shells, bones, wood, rocks and semiprecious stones. Some were coloured with vegetable and animal dyes. Beads which were made by the San bushmen from ostrich eggs, estimated to be between 37 and 39,000 years old, have been found in the Rift Valley of Kenya. A beaded neckpiece found in the tomb of Tutankhamen has been estimated to be 2–3,000 years old.

String of ancient Afghani beads

Lapis lazuli, carnelian and pottery beads, mixed and restrung. Circa 1200 AD

Beads were also seen as having value and were used as a form of currency in some cultures. It is said that in 1626, Manhattan was bought for $24.00-worth of beads! I am not sure how true this story is, but it does indicate the importance of beads as a form of trade, hence the term 'trade beads'.

Lots of different styles of beadwork have been developed in various parts of the world. The Native American Indians are renowned for their brightly coloured beads and the patterns they create with them. So are the Ndebele tribes of Southern Africa and the indigenous people of South America, the Saraguro. The patterns and colours used within their beadwork can be of great significance, conveying messages and establishing marital, economical and tribal status – particularly true of South African beadwork.

Beaded medicine bag

Made in Peyote stitch and lined with fabric. Believed to be about 50 years old. Pakistan/Afghanistan

The use of beads in Europe, from simple stringing to complex bead embroidery, dates back hundreds of years. During the 17th century and the first half of the 18th century, bead embroidery was a recognised craft. Skills were passed from mother to daughter as they created beautiful furnishings and tapestries. Elaborate beaded jewellery using a variety of semiprecious stones and beads were extremely popular in the Victorian era.

Today it seems that the art and craft of beading is making a comeback and is becoming an increasingly popular hobby. Modern beaders have a real advantage over their forebears, as the bead-making industry takes full advantage of modern technologies to offer wonderful beads in thousands of colours, shapes, sizes and finishes.

Martha Edlin's purse

Silk embroidered with beads.
1670's. English.
Reproduced by kind permission of the
Victoria & Albert Museum

Beaded purse

Silk embroidered with beads.
Inscribed: Hit or Miss there it is 1628. *British*
Reproduced by kind permission of the
Victoria & Albert Museum.

Materials

All the materials used for beadwork are readily available from craft outlets and specialist suppliers. I have mentioned all the items needed to create the projects in this book, but I am sure you will soon start adding to these.

Beads

There are many types of beads available, and choosing the right beads for a project is essential. So, I cannot emphasise enough the importance of finding a good supplier who will be able to advise you on the best beads to use. Most beads are sold either by weight (grams) or in hanks. It is impossible to mention every bead available, so I focus on the most common ones.

These larger-than-life images show some of the more common beads. From left to right: Triangle size 8; Czech seed bead, size 10; Delica bead, size 11; and Japanese seed bead, size 11.

Seed beads
These are the most popular type of bead and there are two types.

Japanese beads are cylindrical in shape and range in size from 6 (the largest) to 22 (the smallest). They are thought to be more uniform in size and have larger holes than the equivalent size of Czech bead. They are ideal for all types of beadwork.

Czech beads range in size from 7 to 20. They are usually more doughnut-shaped than Japanese ones, and are best used for off-loom beading and bead embroidery.

Delica (or antique) beads
These superior beads are perfectly cylindrical in shape and have thin walls and large holes. They are ideal for bead weaving where a very flat, smooth finish is required. There are only two sizes: size 11 and the larger size 8. They are more expensive than seed beads, but well worth using for that special project.

Bugle beads
These are long cylindrical beads available in a variety of colours, finishes and twists. They are sized in millimetres, the most common sizes being 2, 3, and 5mm. Take care when using them as they can have quite sharp edges which could cut through thread. They are mainly used for edgings and fringes.

Shaped beads
Apart from the usual cylindrical shape, there are also other shapes of beads– triangles, squares and hexagonal (six sided) – which can give an unusual and different texture.

Faceted beads
Crystals are a good example of faceted beads. They are useful as accent or feature beads, and I use them quite frequently. They are sized in millimetres from 3 to 10mm.

Round beads
These can be made from plastic, wood, glass and semiprecious stones. They are sized in millimetres from 2 to 10mm or even larger.

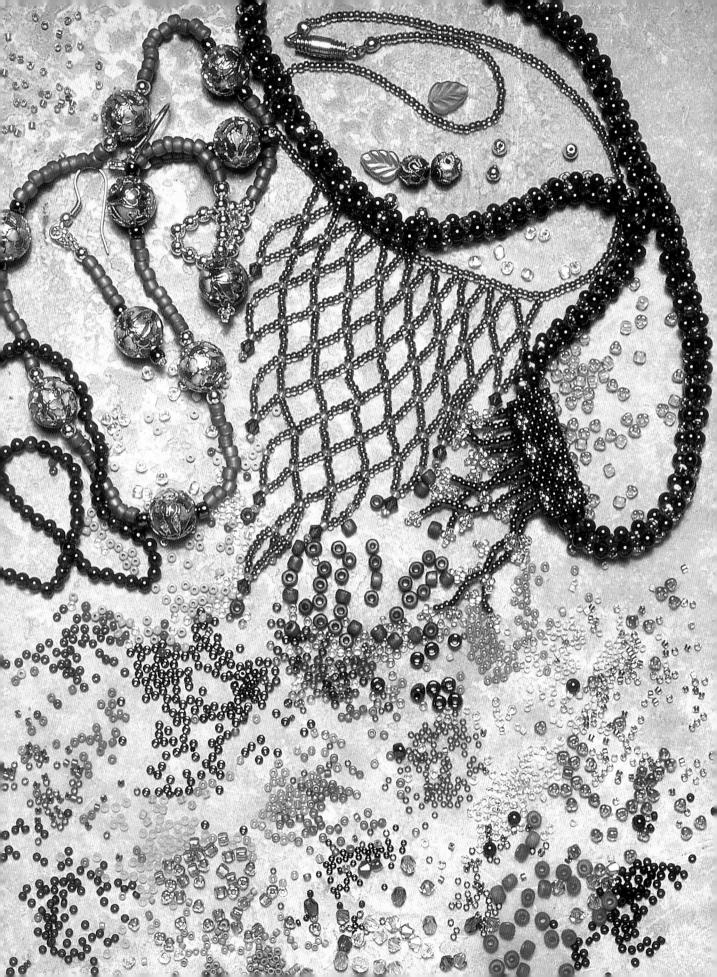

Bead finishes

Descriptions of different finishes vary from one range to another. The following are some of the common terms.

Trans. (transparent)   beads that can be seen through (may have a semi-frosted finish)

Opaque   beads that may have a sheen, but cannot be seen through.

Frosted (or semi-frosted)   semi-transparent beads with a chalky finish

AB (Aurora Borealis, iridescent, or rainbow) multicoloured beads with a transparent, opaque or frosted finish.

Iris   beads with an iridescent metal-like finish (can also appear on frosted beads).

Ceylon (or Lustre)   beads with a uniform, shiny, pearlised finish.

Metallic   beads with a shiny metal-like finish.

Lined   transparent beads with a coloured lining to the holes. Silver lined (S/L) and gold lined (G/L) are the most common, but lots of other colours are available.

Using beads

When using seed or Delica beads do not mix different manufacturers' ranges as this will give an uneven bumpy finish.

Buy enough beads to complete the project, as the colour of your next batch may be slightly different.

Cull beads before starting a project. Discard broken or badly-shaped beads and those with holes that are too small for your needle.

Needles and threads

Any needle which passes through the bead hole can be used, but I recommend you use beading needles. These are long and thin needles in a variety of sizes (10, 12, 13, 15 and 16 (the thinnest). A size 10 needle is used for all the projects in this book. You can also buy a big-eyed needle (one long eye with a point at each end) – useful for those who find threading needles a problem.

There is a wide range of bead stringing materials, but the most popular is Nymo thread, a strong waxed thread (originally developed for the tailoring industry) which is available on 60m (65yd) bobbins or 275m (300yd) spools. It is available in a variety of colours and sizes (00, the finest to FF, the thickest), but you will only need size D for the projects in this book. You can use Silamide, a two-ply waxed nylon thread, although, personally, I think it frays a little more easily than Nymo.

Silk is another versatile thread and comes in a variety of colours and sizes. It knots very easily and is ideal for stringing pearls and other delicate beads.

Pulling the thread through beeswax, lip balm or a proprietry thread conditioner can help prevent the thread fraying.

Preparing threads

Tangles, knots and frayed ends are most frustrating; these tips will help prevent them:

Avoid thread lengths longer than 150cm (60in).

Pull the thread between index finger and thumb several times to straighten it, then pull the thread through a thread conditioner.

Using beading needles

Piercing the thread with the needle is a common problem in beadwork – it weakens the thread and can make your beadwork untidy. Reduce the chance of this happening by blunting the tip of the needle with a fine file.

When threading needles, you will find it easier to hold the thread steady and bring the eye of the needle to the thread, rather than take the thread to the needle.

Use the eye end of the needle, rather than its point, to unpick knotted thread; this lessens the chances of piercing and fraying the thread.

Findings

A general term for necklace clasps, brooch backs, earring wires and studs, jump rings and bead tips, etc. used to finish beaded jewellery. There is a wide choice available.

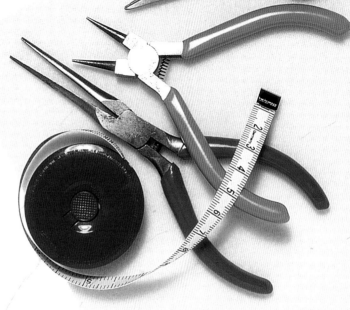

Other equipment

The following items are useful, though not essential additions to your workbox.

Bead mat a piece of velvet, felt or thin sponge that stops beads rolling about.

Flat and round-nosed pliers used to attach findings to bead work.

Measuring tape and sharp **sewing scissors**

Small **pots** or saucers for holding beads.

Basic bead stringing

Bead stringing is perhaps the oldest known form of beading. It is also the easiest as it is just a matter of adding beads on to a length of thread. There are, however, a few techniques which will help make the finished string of beads more secure.

You will need
Eight to twelve 10mm cloisonné feature beads

10g 4mm round beads, gold

Japanese seed beads:
15g size 6, green AB
10g size 6, bronze
Four size 11, gold S/L

Size 10 beading needle
Size D or thicker Nymo thread
Thread conditioner

Earring wires

Necklace and earrings

This project is designed to give you a general *feel* for beads and, to help illustrate the stringing techniques, I have used large cloisonné beads, large seed beads and standard size Nymo thread to make a necklace and a matching set of earrings.

Cloisonné beads are very colourful and their texture contrasts well with the smoothness of the other beads. However, there is no reason why you cannot use different beads; the stringing techniques will still apply.

1. Measure your neck to determine the length of the necklace. Space the cloisonné beads along the required length, then determine the number of the other beads that will fit in the spaces. For this necklace, ten size 6 green seed beads, one size 6 bronze seed bead and one 4mm gold round bead fit in the spaces.

2. Cut a 115cm (45in) length of thread, pull it across the block of the thread conditioner two or three times, then thread it through the needle.

3. Pick up one green seed bead, then pass the needle through the bead again to create a temporary stopper bead.

4. Position the stopper bead approximately 30cm (12in) from one end of the thread and pull the thread tight. Pick up a further nine green seed beads, then slide them along to the stopper bead.

5. Pick up a bronze seed bead, a cloissoné bead and another bronze seed bead, then pass them along the thread.

6. Pick up ten green seed beads, pass them along the thread, then pick up a gold bead, a cloissoné bead and another gold round bead.

7. Pass the beads to the other end of thread to complete the basic stringing pattern.

8. Repeat the basic stringing pattern (steps 5–7), until you have the required length of necklace.

9. Release the stopper bead by taking the tail end of the thread back through the bead.

10. Thread on thirteen gold round beads, then take the thread back through the first of these.

11. Pull the thread through to form a closure loop of gold beads, then start passing the needle and thread back through the string of beads.

12. Tie a knot between the beads at intervals along the string; start each knot by passing the needle under the thread between two beads . . .

13. . . . pull the thread to form an open loop, pass the needle through the underside of the loop . . .

14. . . . then pull the thread to close the knot. For extra security, you can apply a dab of clear nail varnish on each knot. Here I have moved some of the beads along the string to show the knot.

15. Continue passing the thread back through the beads, knotting it at intervals. At the end of the string, you will have two threads coming out of the last green bead.

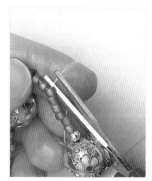

16. Thread five gold round beads and a cloisonné bead on one of the threads, then add four size 11, silver-lined gold beads. Pass the needle back through the first of these . . .

17. . . . then through the cloisonné bead. Pull the thread taut to create a four-bead stopper. Take the thread back through the string of beads, knotting at intervals (see steps 12–14).

18. Now take the other thread through the five gold round beads, the cloisonné bead and the four stopper beads and back through the cloisonné bead. Take the thread right through the rest of the string, again knotting it at intervals.

19. Pass both threads through the closure loop beads and back through a 5–7cm (2–3in) length of the string of beads. Trim off the excess thread to complete the necklace.

The finished necklace and matching earrings

The earrings were strung and knotted at intervals in much the same way as the necklace. The stringing consists of one cloisonné bead, five size 6, green seed beads, one size 6, bronze seed bead and one 4mm, gold round bead.

Four size 11, silver-lined gold seed beads act as a stopper at the bottom of the string and nine 4mm, gold round beads form the loop for the earring wires.

Netting

Netting has a lovely open weave that is useful for edging and finishing. During the Victorian era, it was very popular for necklaces, and for edging clothes and soft furnishings. There are two basic types of netting: vertical netting, which, as its name implies, is woven up and down; and horizontal netting, which is woven from side to side. Both types are flexible and versatile. The principal structure of netting patterns is a series of short strings of the same colour beads with contrasting connector beads.

You will need

Japanese seed beads, size 11:
20g brown AB
10g alabaster-lined salmon
Nine 4mm bi-cone faceted crystal light brown
Size 10 beading needle
Size D Nymo thread in complementary colour
Thread conditioner
Screw clasp
Two bead tips

Netted necklace

This lovely netted necklace, worked up in brown and salmon beads, is a typical example of the basic structure of vertical netting. At the end of this project I have included some variations of vertical netting and a very simple horizontal netted necklace in gorgeous gold and mauve iris beads

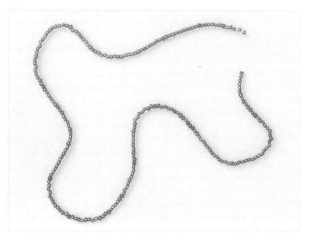

1. Cut a 115cm (45in) length of thread, wax it, then string a row of the brown AB seed beads to the required length of the necklace.

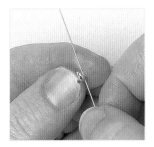

2. Take one end of the thread through the hole in a bead tip . . .

3. . . . thread on another brown AB seed bead and take the needle back through the hole in the bead tip and some of the beads on the string.

4. Pull the thread through until the bead is sitting in the cup of the bead tip.

5. Use a pair of flat-nosed pliers to close the bead tip round the bead. Referring to page 16, take the thread back through the string of beads, knotting it at intervals.

6. Add the clasp to the open ring on the bead tip, then use round-nosed pliers to close the ring. Repeat steps 2–6 at the other end of the string. You should now have three lengths of thread through the beads, and a loose thread at each end. Referring to page 16, pass these ends back through a 5–7.5cm (2–3in) length of the string, then trim off the excess threads.

7. Fold the string of beads in half, locate the centre bead and count twenty-five beads back to one side of the centre bead. Pass the needle (with a new length of thread) through the twenty-fifth bead, leaving a 15cm (6in) tail to be woven in later.

8. Begin the netting by threading the following beads on to the needle: five brown seed beads, one salmon, five brown, one salmon, five brown, one salmon, one crystal and one salmon.

9. Pull the beads up to the string, take the thread round the bottom salmon bead and up through the crystal and the next salmon bead.

10. Thread on five brown, one salmon and five brown seed beads, then take the needle through the second salmon bead up the net.

11. Pull the thread through, add five brown seed beads, then take the needle through the fifth bead to the right of the start bead.

12. Pull the thread through the bead to complete the first column of netting. This forms the basic design of the net.

13. Add five brown, one salmon and five brown seed beads, then take the needle and thread through the second salmon bead on the left-hand side of the net.

14. Repeat steps 8–10 to form the bottom shape of the second column of the netting.

15. Repeat steps 10–11 to complete the second column of netting.

16. Repeat steps 13–15 to extend the netting across the string of beads, then, for the bottom shape of the centre column, add five brown, one salmon, five brown, one salmon, **nine** brown, one salmon, one crystal and one salmon bead.

17. Repeat step 9, then add nine brown, one salmon and five brown beads and take the needle through the second salmon up the left-hand side of the net.

18. Take the thread round the salmon bead and back down through the five brown beads and the next salmon bead.

19. Thread on three brown and four salmon beads, then take the needle back through the first of the salmon beads.

20. Pull the thread tight to form a small loop of salmon beads. Add three brown beads, then take the needle through the salmon bead on the left-hand side of the net and up through the five brown and the next salmon bead.

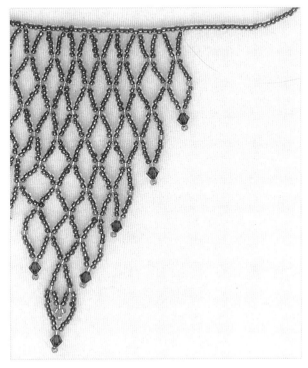

21. Reverse the pattern to complete the right-hand side of the netting. Complete the project by weaving and knotting all loose threads back through the beading, then trimming off all excess thread.

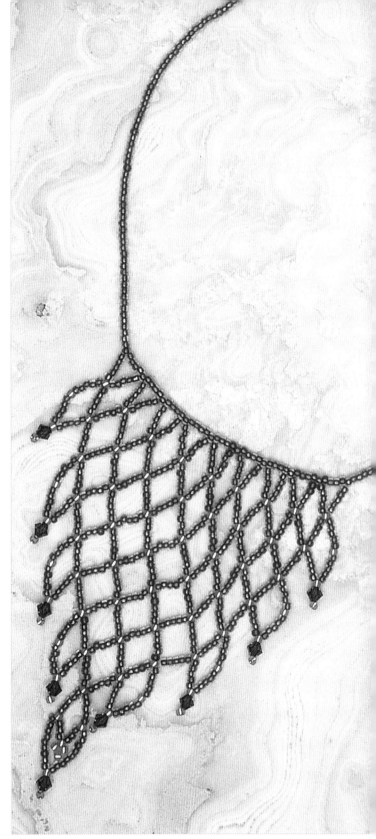

The finished necklace

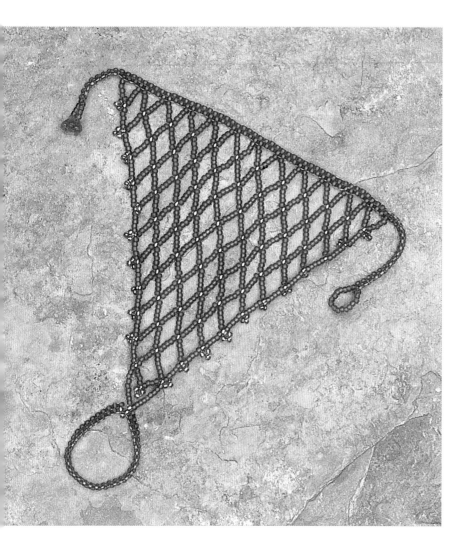

Hand tanga

This piece is really a bracelet-sized version of the project necklace, but with closed sides. The wrist strap and finger loop are two-bead-wide (one bead per row) Peyote stitch bands (see page 24). The length of both bands must be sized to allow a little give but they must not be too loose. The netting begins twenty-one beads to one side of the centre point of the wrist band.

1. Pick up five main, one contrast, five main and one contrast bead. Take the thread round the bottom contrast bead, then back through five main beads and the other contrast bead.

2. Pick up five main beads and take the thread through the third bead along on the wrist strap.

3. Pick up five main, one contrast and five main beads, then take the thread down through the bottom contrast bead of the previous row to close the side of the net.

4. Repeat step 1.

5. Pick up five main, one contrast and five main beads, then take the thread back up through the contrast bead on the previous row.

6. Repeat step 2.

7. Continue working steps 1–6, increasing the depth by working step 3 two times in the next row, three times in the next etc. When you reach the middle of the net, string on the finger ring and add the centre detail. Decorate the sides of the net with three-bead picot edging (see page 29).

Japanese seed beads size 11:
15g dark amethyst trans. A/B
5g light amethyst matte trans.
One feature bead for clasp

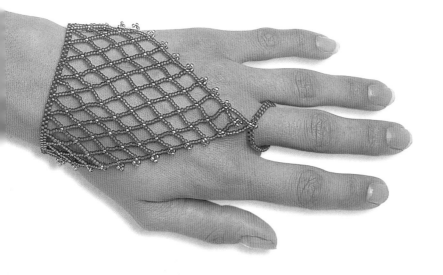

Japanese seed beads, size 11:
20g, dark amethyst trans. A/B
10g, crystal S/L
19, 4mm bi-cone crystals, smokey grey
Bead tips & clasp

Three-net necklace

The neckline for this necklace is made in much the same way as the project piece, but the net is made into three parts by increasing and decreasing it across the string of beads. Begin the netting fifty-four beads to one side of the centre point. A small triangular shape, closed with a seven-bead string (three dark amethyst, one crystal and three dark amethyst), links the sides of each net.

Detail showing the small triangle shapes used to link the sides of the net.

Peyote stitch

Peyote stitch (also known as gourd stitch, twill stitch or diagonal weave) is often associated with native American and African beadwork. Its popularity with beaders is due to the fact that the stitch is extremely versatile and can be worked up quite quickly. I have used flat, even-count Peyote stitch for the projects in this book. Consistent tension across the beadwork is very important. If the tension is too loose the beads will not sit correctly and gaps may appear, if it is too tight the work may bunch up and wrinkle.

You will need
Japanese seed beads, size 11:
20g cobalt opaque
5g turquoise opaque
5g maroon opaque
5g yellow opaque
Eleven 4mm bi-cone turquoise crystals
Size 10 beading needle
Size D Nymo thread
Thread conditioner
Magnetic necklace clasp

Blue choker

This choker is a simple, four-bead-wide (two beads per row) Peyote stitch neck band decorated with a fringed pendant. I have used the vibrant colours that are a common feature of Native American beadwork.

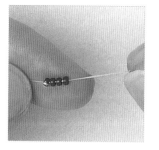 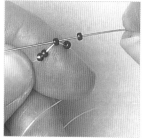

1. Referring to pages 14 and 15, prepare a 115cm (45in) length of thread and create a stopper knot with a cobalt bead, then add three more cobalt beads. These will form the first two rows of the neck band. Anchor the tail end of the thread firmly between your index and second finger to help maintain tension.

2. Now start weaving to create the first three rows of Peyote stitch. Pick up another cobalt bead, then, working left to right, pass the needle back through the last-but-one bead.

3. Pull the thread taut so that the new bead is sitting on top of the last of the first four beads added. These two beads are now in row three and one respectively.

4. Pick up another bead, and, still working right to left, take the thread through the first of the first four beads.

5. Pull the thread tight to complete the third row and create the staggered pattern of this stitch – one bead up and one bead down.

6. Flatten the beadwork with your thumb and index finger and loop the thread between your index and second fingers to keep the work taut. Add a blue bead then pass the thread, left to right, through the last up bead of the third row.

7. Add another bead and pass the needle through the other up bead on the row, then pull the thread tight again.

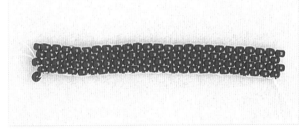

8. Continue building up the neck band by repeating steps 2–7 (adding two beads on each row).

9. When the thread gets short, start a new length by passing it through a bead a few rows back down the neck band . . .

10. . . . pass the needle under the thread between two beads to form a loop, then make a knot.

11. Weave the thread up the beadwork, knotting it around the thread path. Bring the new thread out through the same bead as the old thread. Following the thread path, weave and knot the short thread back down the beadwork.

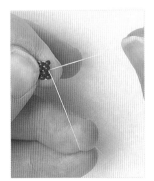

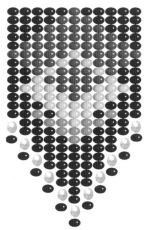

Fringe pattern

12. When the neck band is long enough, fold it in half to find the middle bead and count back five beads (to the left). Pass a new 115cm (45in) length of thread through the fifth bead.

13. Pull the thread to leave a 15cm (6in) tail, then, referring to the pattern (left), thread on the first string of beads.

14. Take thread round the bottom bead, then back up through the rest of the string and the bead on the neck band. Take the thread down through an adjacent bead on the neck band.

17. Take the needle and thread through the bead on the other side of the neck band, then pull the thread to close the loop. Weave the thread through the loop two or three times then weave and knot the thread back into the neck band.

15. Repeat steps 13–14 to complete the fringe strings, then weave and knot the ends of thread into the neck band.

16. Release the stopper thread at the start end of the neck band, then pick up four beads, the magnetic clasp and four more beads

18. Fit the other end of the neck band to the magnetic clasp in the same way to complete the choker, then add a few fringe strings.

Finished blue choker

Ring

This attractive ring is worked as an eight-bead-wide (four beads per row) Peyote stitch band, sized to fit your finger. I chose this piece to show you how to follow Peyote stitch patterns and introduce other colours into the work. The more even-sized Delica beads are best for this type of work.

You will need

Delica beads, size 11:
1g purple iris
1g gold S/L

Size 10 beading needle
Size D Nymo black thread
Thread conditioner

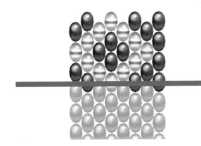

Pattern for ring motif

Peyote stitch patterns can be worked from the bottom up or the top down. Use a ruler to follow a pattern, moving it up (or down) half a bead at a time. On wide complex patterns, count the number of beads of each colour for a row and set them to one side – then, if you run out of a colour before you reach the end of a row, you know you have made a mistake somewhere!

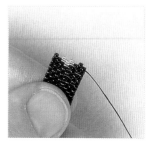

1. Referring to page 24, but starting with a string of eight purple iris beads, work up a four-beads-per-row band of Peyote stitch the length of which should be sized for the recipient's finger (here the length allows for the motif to be added).

2. Referring to page 27, start working the pattern. Working right to left, add a purple iris, a purple iris, a gold and a purple iris bead for the next row.

3. Now, working left to right, add a purple iris, a gold, a gold and another purple iris bead.

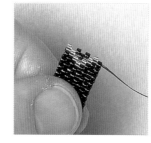

4. On the third row, add a purple iris, a gold, a purple iris and a gold.

5. On the fourth row, add a gold, a purple iris, a purple iris and a gold.

6. Now work the other half of the motif, the last row of which is worked right to left with a purple iris, a purple iris, a gold and a purple iris bead. Check the fit on the finger and, if necessary, add an *even* number of plain rows of purple iris.

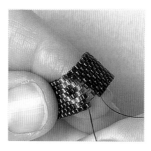

7. Fold the band in half and align the high beads at one end with the low beads at the other.

8. Take the working thread, that comes out of the low bead in the front, through first high bead on the back.

9. Now take the thread through all the high beads, alternating between the back edge to front edge. Pull the thread tight to 'zip up' the two ends.

10. Weave the thread through the beads and snip off the excess. Weave in a new length of thread and exit through the gold bead on the edge of the motif.

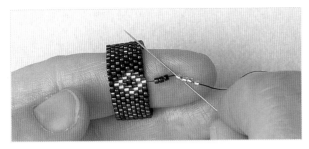
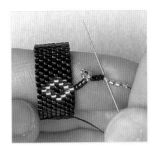

11. Pick up three purple iris beads and four gold ones, then take the needle back through the first of the gold beads added.

12. Pull the thread tight to form a small cluster, thread on three purple iris and another four gold beads and take the needle back through the first of these gold beads.

13. Now take the thread back through just the six purple iris beads.

14. Pull the thread tight, take it up through the gold bead on the edge of motif (to complete the first fringe), then down through an adjacent purple iris bead.

15. Repeat steps 11–13 to form a second fringe. Weave the thread across to exit at the other side of the centre fringe and add a third fringe. Weave the thread into the beadwork and trim off the excess.

16. Weave a new length of thread to exit at an edge bead adjacent to one side of the fringe.

17. Add three gold beads and take the needle up through the next bead along the band.

18. Pull the thread tight to form the first cluster of the picot edge, then take the needle and thread down through the next adjacent edge bead. Repeat steps 17–18 to add picot edging right round the band to the other side of the fringe.

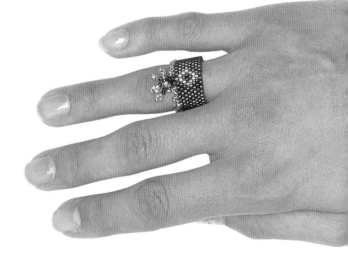

The finished ring

Pink and grey ring

This ring is made in much the same way as the project. The eight-bead-wide (four beads per row) grey strip is worked first, then the pattern is decreased to four beads wide (two beads per row) at each end.

Delica beads, size 11:
1g grey trans. iris
1g old rose

Peyote stitch pattern

Join the pink ends together (see page 28), then manually work the pink beads to form a diagonal strip.

White ring

This is a plain six-bead-wide (three beads per row) strip of pearl white beads joined together as shown on page 28. Picot edging, worked with lavender beads, is sewn to both sides of the ring. Four little fringes, worked with frosted white rondelles, protrude from the centre of the band.

Delica beads, size 11:
1g pearl white
1g lavender
Four 4mm frosted white rondelles

Dark blue and red ring

This six-bead-wide (three beads per row) band is very similar in design to the ring shown on pages 27–29. A tiny fringe emphasises the diamond motif and one side of the ring is finished with a picot edge.

Delica beads, size 11:
1g red lustre
1g blue iris

Peyote stitch pattern

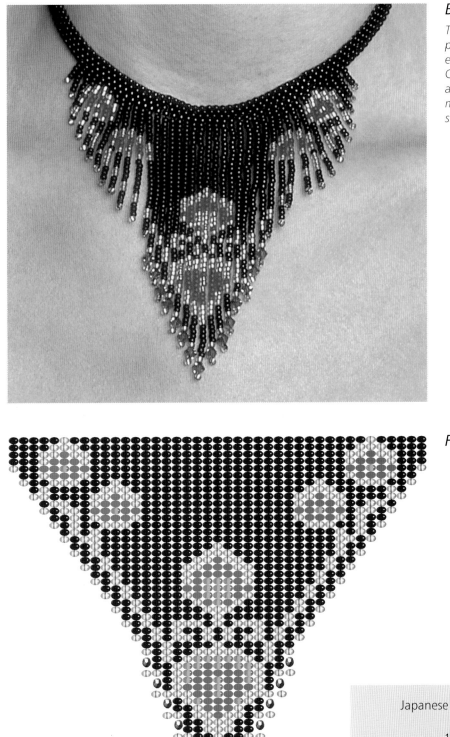

Black choker

This classic little black piece is perfect for that special evening out. It was inspired by Charles Rene Macintosh roses and is worked in the same manner as the blue choker shown on pages 24–27.

Fringe pattern

Japanese seed beads, size 11
20g black
10g gold S/L
10g frosted matt red
5g lime green lustre
Fifteen, bi-cone 4mm crystals smokey grey

Iris tapestry

This wall hanging would look good on any wall. It is a large project, but well worth the effort. On Peyote stitch pieces such as this, it is always best to set aside the number of each colour of bead required for a row rather than work from your bulk stock of each colour. Working this way, you will soon know if you make a mistake.

Start the piece from the bottom of the pattern, threading a string of fifty beads for the first two rows. Move up the pattern half a bead at a time

For clarity, the pattern has been split into two parts and the common row on each part is marked with a red line.

The two tabs that support the hanging on the brass rod are twelve-bead-wide (six beads per row) extension strips woven at the top of the pattern. These are turned over and their ends are sewn to the back of the hanging in much the same way as the ends of the rings shown on the previous pages are joined together.

Japanese seed beads, size 11
30g white gold lined
3g light grey trans.
3g blue iris
20g bronze alabaster silver lined
1g yellow Ceylon
2g medium green opaque
3g violet alabaster silver lined
3g yellow green lined
4g emerald green yellow lined
1green trans. AB
5g deep blue silver lined
2g chartruese opaque
1g light gold crystal AB

Small tapestry pole

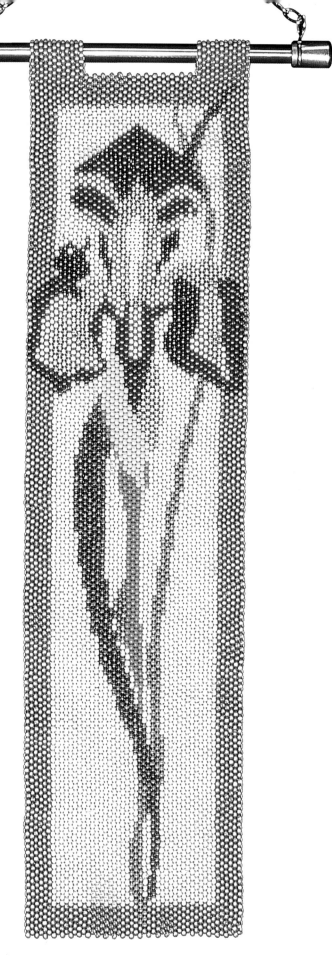

Peyote stitch pattern
The red lines denote the common row of beads.

Brick stitch

This stitch gets its name from its resemblance to the pattern of brick walls. It is also known as Comanche stitch, as it was (and still is) one of the main techniques used by native Americans along with Peyote stitch. The firm, even finish makes this a very popular stitch with beaders, especially for small projects such as earrings. It is slower to work up than Peyote stitch, for example, but I find it very versatile, particularly for increasing and decreasing.

Ruby earrings

These earrings are quick and fun to make. In this first earring project I show you how to create a triangular shape by increasing the number of beads in each row. Follow the pattern and set aside the quantity of each colour for each row (see page 32).

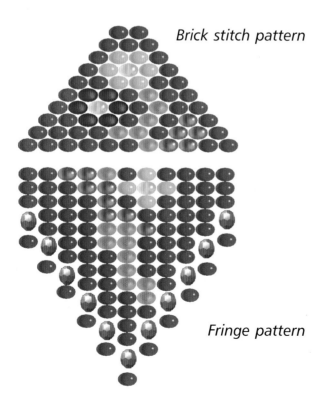

Brick stitch pattern

Fringe pattern

You will need

Delica beads, size 11:
1g old rose
1g sapphire
1g green
2g cranberry
1g green trans.
1g yellow trans.

Eleven 4mm bi-cone crystals pale pink

Size 10 beading needle
Size D Nymo thread
Thread conditioner
Earring hook findings

1. Pick up two cranberry beads, then take the thread round and back through both beads.

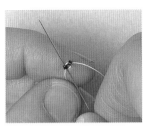

2. Pull the thread through, then take needle back through the first bead again.

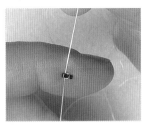

3. Pull the thread tight. The two beads will now sit side by side.

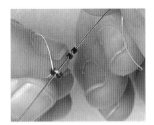

4. Pick up two more beads, then take the needle under the thread linking the two beads in the last row.

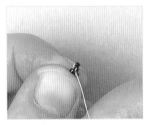

5. Pull the thread through the beads . . .

6. . . . then move the top of the first bead in this row down to the left-hand side.

7. Now take the thread back up through the second bead of the second row.

8. Pull the thread through, add another bead, then take the needle under the linking thread between the two beads in the first row.

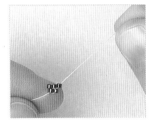

9. Take the thread back up through the last bead and pull tight to finish the second row.

10. Working back across the work, pick up a cranberry and an old rose bead and take the needle under the thread linking the two right-hand beads in the second row.

11. Pull the thread through and push the cranberry bead down to the right-hand side. Pick up an old rose bead, then take the needle under the thread between the first two beads on the row below.

12. Pull the thread through, take it back up through the old rose bead and pull it tight. Pick up a cranberry bead, then take the needle under the same linking thread as in step 11.

13. Take the thread up through the cranberry bead and tighten it to complete the third row.

14. Referring to the pattern on page 32, repeat steps 10–13, working back and forth, until the brick stitch design is complete.

15. Now add the loop for the earring wire. Pick up nine cranberry beads on the tail thread, then take the needle down through the bead next to that from which the thread exits.

16. Pull the thread to form a loop, then take the thread back up through the first bead of the first row.

17. Pass the thread through all nine loop beads, down through the second bead in the first row, up through the first bead and back through the loop beads. Repeat again for extra security, then weave the thread through the beadwork and trim off excess.

18. Referring to the pattern on page 34, and the instructions on page 26, add the fringing.

19. Use the round-nosed pliers to close the loop on the earring finding on to the loop on the beadwork. The finished pair of earrings is shown on page 38.

Brown & gold earrings

This is another triangular-shaped earring, but here, the triangle is worked from the wide base up to the point. This simple example illustrates ladder stitch, which is used as the first row of brick stitch, and the technique of decreasing the number of beads in each row. Follow the pattern, row by row.

Brick stitch pattern

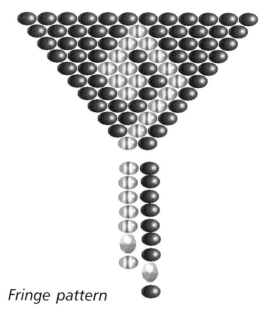

Fringe pattern

You will need

Delica beads, size 11:
2g brown iris
2g gold S/L
Four 4mm bi-cone crystals, topaz
Size 10 beading needle
Size D Nymo thread
Thread conditioner
Earring stud findings

1. Referring to steps 1–3 on page 33, set two brown beads side by side, then take the needle and thread down through the second bead.

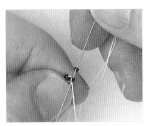

2. Pull the thread through, pick up another brown bead, then take the needle round and down through the previous bead.

3. Pull the thread tight, setting the new bead by the side of the previous one. Take the thread up through the new bead, down through the previous one, up the new one and pull it tight.

4. Repeat step 2, but, this time, take the needle round and *up* through the previous bead. Repeat step 3 but take the thread *down* the new bead, *up* the previous one and back *down* through the new one.

5. Repeat steps 2–4 until you have twelve beads in the row of ladder stitch.

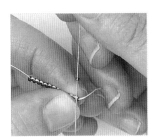

6. Turn the row, so that the working thread is coming up out of the top of the last bead, then start to decrease. Pick up a bead, then take the needle under the threads linking the last two beads of the previous row.

7. Pull the thread through then take it back up through the new bead. Pull the thread tight so that the new bead sits between the last two in the previous row.

8. Add a new bead and, working back across the work, repeat steps 6–7.

9. Referring to the pattern, repeat step 8 until you have eleven beads in the row.

10. Build up the design until you have just two beads in the final row. Add two fringes (see page 26) and a seven-bead loop (see page 36) for the stud.

The two projects and a pair of black and silver earrings

11. Finally, use the round-nosed pliers to secure the stud to the loop. Set the stud in each earring so that the gold string of the fringe is nearest the face.

Black and silver earrings

These earrings are simple rectangles of brick stitch with the same number of beads on each row. Begin by making an eight-bead ladder, then start each row of brick stitch as steps 4–7 on page 37, but end it when eight beads have been added. Finish the earrings by adding the loop and findings of your choice.

Delica beads, size 11
2g crystal S/L
2g gunmetal

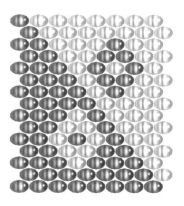

Brick stitch pattern

Brick stitch bracelet

This elegant bracelet combines both the increasing and decreasing techniques used to make the earring projects on the previous pages. I used a magnetic clasp to finish the bracelet, but, of course, you can use another type of clasp.

Start the beadwork at this end.

Delica beads, size 11
2g gunmetal
2g grey trans. AB

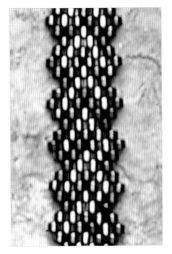

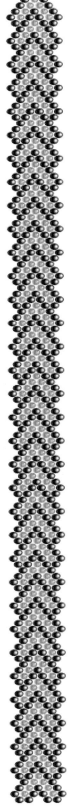

Right-angle weave

Right-angle weave (or RAW) has a lovely fluid open structure that builds up quickly. Each bead sits at a right angle to the other and the thread passes at right angles to join the beads.

Bracelet

This first right-angle weave project is a simple bracelet made with bugle beads and some lovely triangle AB beads. These particular beads emphasise the structure of this stitch. The bracelet has a triangular cross-section.

You will need
15g 3mm bugle, cream matt
15g triangle, size 8, champagne AB
1g Japanese seed bead, size 11, frosted garnet

Size 10 beading needle
Size D Nymo thread
Thread wax

Bracelet clasp, spring clasp and jump ring
Bead tips

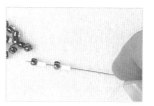

1. Pick up one bugle, one triangle, one bugle and one triangle bead.

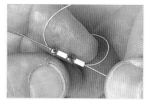

2. Pull the thread through the beads to leave a 25cm (10in) tail, then take the thread round and back through all four beads again.

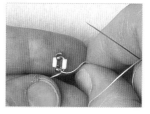

3. Pull the thread to form a square shape, with the bugle beads vertical, and with the working thread over the tail thread. This square will form one side of the triangle pattern.

4. Take the working thread up through the right-hand bugle bead and pull it through.

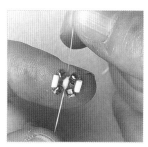

5. Pull the thread tight, pick up a triangle, a bugle and a triangle and take the thread round and back up through the right-hand bugle.

6. Pull the thread tight to form another square shape beside the first. We now have two sides of the triangular cross, side by side.

7. Take the thread through the top right-hand triangle bead and down through the right-hand bugle bead.

8. Pick up a triangle bead and take the thread up through the left-hand bugle bead.

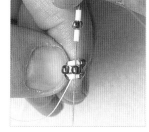

9. Pull the thread tight to close the bottom row of triangle beads, pick up another triangle bead and take the thread down through the right-hand bugle bead.

10. Pull the thread tight then take it right to left through the bottom triangle, up through the left-hand bugle, then left to right through the top triangle bead.

11. Pull the thread tight, pick up one bugle, one triangle and one bugle, then take the thread round and through the last triangle.

12. Pull the thread tight, then take it round and up through the new right-hand bugle bead.

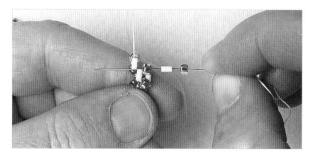
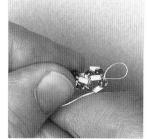
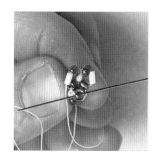

13. Rotate the work clockwise (as viewed from the top) so that the bugle bead is on the left-hand side, pick up one triangle and one bugle then take the thread through the top triangle of the row below.

14. Take the thread up through the left-hand bugle, left to right through the triangle, then down through the new right-hand bugle.

15. Pull the thread tight, rotate the work clockwise again, then take the thread across through the last triangle of the previous row.

16. Pull the thread tight to close the bottom of this row, then take the thread up through the new right-hand bugle. Pick up a triangle then take the thread down through the left-hand bugle bead.

17. Pull the thread tight to close the second row of beads, then take the thread back (left to right) through the lower triangle, up through the right-hand bugle and across (left to right) through the top triangle to start the next sequence.

18. Pick up a bugle, triangle and bugle, take the thread round through the last triangle and pull the thread tight. This square of beads forms the first side of the next row of the pattern.

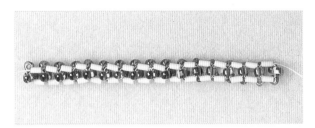

19. Continue building up the length of the bracelet by repeating steps 12–17.

20. Pick up a seed bead on the tail thread and take the thread through an adjacent triangle bead.

21. Pull the thread tight, pick up another seed bead and take the thread through the next adjacent triangle. Repeat with a third seed bead and pull the thread tight. These beads change the shape of the end of the rope from square to circular.

22. Take the thread through the first seed bead, pick up another seed bead and take the thread through the next adjacent seed bead.

23. Pull the thread tight, pick up a seed bead and take the thread through the next adjacent seed bead. Add another bead and pull the thread tight.

24. Repeat steps 22–23 to add three more seed beads. Pick up a bead tip and a seed bead then take the thread round the seed bead and back through the bead tip. Weave the thread back into the rope, then trim the off excess thread.

25. Repeat step 24 to add a bead tip at the other end of the bracelet, then, referring to page 19 add the clasp.

The finished bracelet

Spectacles case

This chic spectacles case uses the same basic RAW technique but, here, it is worked flat. The combination of cream bugle beads and gold seed beads gives this piece an air of sophistication. I lined this beadwork with a piece of linen, but, you could use any material of your choice.

You will need

25g bugle beads, 3mm cream matte
25g Japanese seed beads, size 11, gold S/L

10g Delica beads, size 11, cream matte
One 8mm feature bead
Two 6mm feature bead

Fabric for liner

Size 10 beading needle
Size D Nymo thread
Thread conditioner

1. Pick up eight beads: a bugle, a gold, a bugle, a gold, a bugle, a gold, a bugle and a gold.

2. Take the thread round and back through all eight beads, leaving a 25cm (10in) tail.

3. Pull the thread tight to create a square shape with a bugle bead on each side and a gold bead in each corner.

4. Take the working thread through the bottom bugle, a gold and the right-hand bugle to exit opposite the tail.

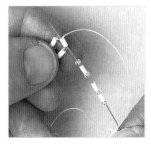

5. Pick up seven beads: a gold, a bugle, a gold, a bugle, a gold, a bugle and a gold. Bring the thread round and pass the needle up through the right-hand bugle of the first square.

6. Pull the thread tight to close the second square.

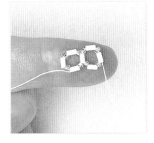

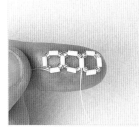

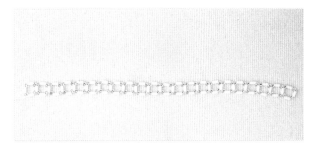

7. Take the working thread clockwise round through a gold, the top bugle, a gold and down through the new right-hand vertical bugle.

8. Thread on seven beads: a gold, a bugle, a gold, a bugle, a gold, a bugle and a gold, then pass the thread round and down through the last vertical bugle.

9. Repeat steps 2–7 until you have made twenty-two squares along the row, then pass the thread round though the beads to exit at the top of the right-hand bugle bead.

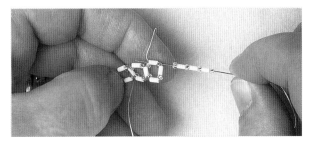

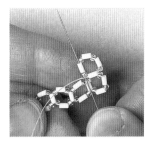

10. Take the thread across through the gold bead and a horizontal bugle, pick up seven beads – a gold, a bugle, a gold, a bugle, a gold, a bugle and a gold – then take the thread round and back through the horizontal bugle on the previous row.

11. Pull the thread tight to form the first square of the next row.

12. Pass the thread up through the gold and left-hand bugle of the new square.

13. Pick up five beads: a gold, a bugle, a gold, a bugle and a gold – then pass the thread left to right through the top horizontal bugle on the row below.

14. Pull the thread to close this square (note that a gold bead is missing from bottom right-hand corner).

15. Pick up a gold bead, then take the needle and thread up through the right-hand vertical bugle of this square.

16. Pull the thread tight to complete this square of the pattern.

17. Pass the thread left to right through the gold, the horizontal bugle and a gold, then down through the left-hand vertical bugle. Pick up another gold bead and pass the needle through the horizontal bugle on the row below.

18. Pull the thread tight, pick up five beads – a gold, a bugle, a gold, a bugle and a gold – then pass the needle down through the left-hand bugle of the previous square on this row.

19. Pass the thread right to left through a gold, the horizontal bugle and a gold, then up through the left-hand vertical bugle. Pull the thread tight again to complete this square.

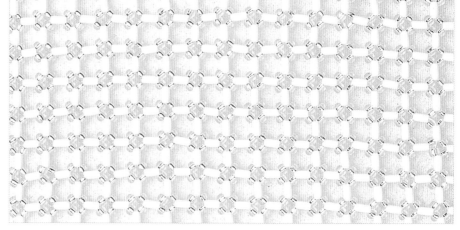

20. Repeat steps 13–19 to complete the second row, then repeat all the steps up to this stage until the beadwork is twenty-three rows deep. Weave the thread back into the beadwork and trim off the excess.

21. Weave a new thread into the beadwork to exit at a corner, then start the triangular flap by working two rows of ten squares. You now have to decrease. Weave the thread horizontally across the top row of gold and bugles to exit at the left-hand side of the second horizontal bugle.

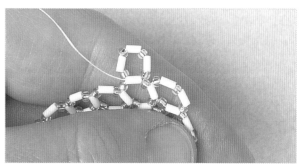

22. Pull the thread through, pick up seven beads – a gold, a bugle, a gold, a bugle, a gold, a bugle and a gold – then take the thread round and back through the horizontal bugle in the row below. Pull the thread tight to form the first square on this row.

23. Work across the row, stopping it one square from the end of the row below. Continue building up the triangular shape as shown here. Complete the flap by making a thirty-bead loop between the two squares of the top row.

24. Now sew the sides together. Weave a new length of thread to exit at the top corner of the front of the case. Pick three beads – a gold, a bugle and a gold – then take the thread down through the vertical bugle at the top of the back of the case.

25. Pull the thread tight to close the beads across the top of the side of the case.

26. Pick up three beads – a gold, a bugle and a gold – then pass the thread up through the front vertical bugle and pull the thread tight to form a complete square of beads.

27. Pass the thread through a gold, a bugle, a gold, a bugle, a gold and a bugle. Pick up a gold bead, then pass the thread down through the next vertical bugle on the front.

28. Pull the thread tight, pick up a gold, a bugle and a gold bead, then pass the thread up through the next bugle on the back of the case. Pick a gold bead and pass the thread through the horizontal bugle on the square above. Take the thread round the square to exit through the last horizontal bugle. Continue down the side and across the bottom of the case.

29. Prepare a liner, then tack this inside the case.

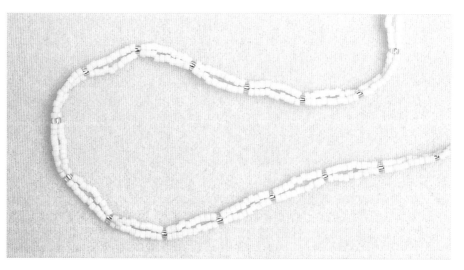

30. Use the 10mm decorative bead and gold seed beads to form a tasselled clasp on the front of the case.

31. Referring to pages 14–16, prepare a double string of beads as shown here. Thread on an 8mm feature bead at each end, then sew the string to the sides of the case.

Opposite
The finished spectacles case

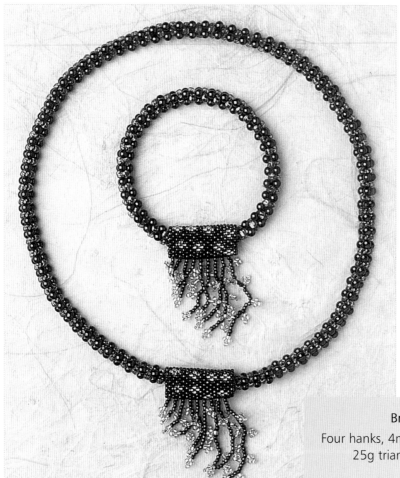

Bracelet and necklace set

This bracelet and necklace set is made in exactly the same way as the RAW project bracelet, using semiprecious garnets and triangle beads. It has a clever little Peyote-stitch slider, decorated with fringing to cover the clasp . The holes in semiprecious stones can be irregular, so, before starting a project, check that the hole in each bead is big enough to take your needle; you may have to cull more beads than usual.

Referring to the ring project pages 26 and 29, and following the pattern below, make a twenty-bead-wide (ten beads per row) block of Peyote stitch for each slider. Sew the ends together, setting the high beads on one end between those on the other. Then, referring to page 26, add the irregular fringing.

Bracelet and necklace
Four hanks, 4mm semiprecious garnets (rounds)
25g triangle, size 8, fuschia-lined AB

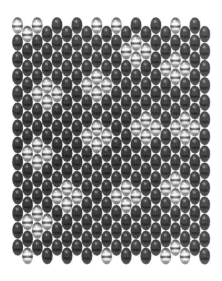

Peyote stitch pattern for slider

Two sliders
Japanese seed beads, size 11
10g ruby red AB
5g gold S/L

Rhapsody in blue

This piece, inspired by the music of George Gershwin, is made with blue iris, bronze and gold seed beads. The bead pendant is encased in Peyote stitch. It has a picot edging and a brick-stitch feature. The right-angle weave rope is worked up with size 11 seed beads.

Herringbone stitch

This stitch gets its name from the fact that it resembles a piece of knitted fabric. It is often associated with beadwork made by the Ndebele tribe of South Africa.

In common with Peyote stitch, you start herringbone stitch by stringing the beads for the first two rows, then weave the stitch with the beads for the third row. Tension is all important, especially at the start, so wrap the tail thread round your little finger and hold the work tightly between your thumb and index finger to keep the tension correct.

You will need

Japanese seed beads, size 11:
40g blue semi-matte trans.
2g dark red semi-matte trans.
1g grey/blue Ceylon
1g light gold crystal AB

Size 10 beading needle
Size D Nymo white thread
Thread conditioner

Hook-and-loop fastener

Purse

This small purse is worked up as a flat panel which is then folded to form the front, the back and the flap. Small pieces of hook-and-loop fastener are used to secure the flap. The purse can be lined with fabric if desired.

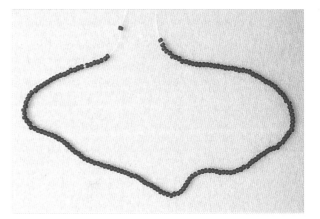

1. Thread on a stopper bead (see page 15) then add 164 blue beads. These will form the first two rows of the purse, starting at the bottom left-hand corner of the pattern.

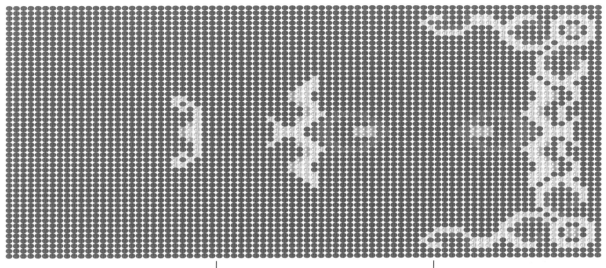

Herringbone stitch pattern | *fold line* | *fold line*

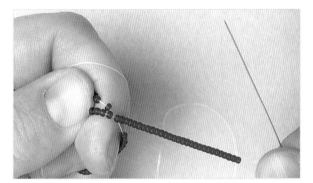

2. You must maintain tension with this stitch, so wind the tail end of the string of beads round your finger to leave a short working length.

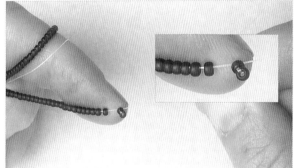

3. Referring to the right-hand end of the third row of the pattern, pick up one blue bead, pass the needle through the end bead on the string, then pull the thread tight.

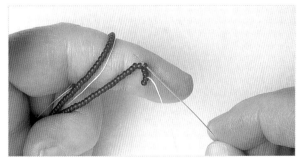

4. Miss two beads on the string, then take the needle through the next loose bead on the string.

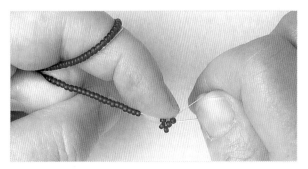

5. Pull both the tail and working threads tight to create the start of the herringbone structure.

6. Pick up a blue and a gold bead and take the needle and thread through the next loose bead on the string.

7. Pull the thread through and tighten both ends again.

8. Holding the beaded pattern taut, miss two beads on the string and pass the thread through the next loose bead.

9. Pull both threads tight to close the beadwork.

10. Pick up two gold beads and take the needle through the next loose bead on the string.

11. Pull the thread through and tighten the beadwork again.

12. Following the pattern, repeat steps 4–11 across the full width of the piece, pulling both threads as you work to keep the beads in their correct positions.

13. Hold the stopper-bead end of the work tight, pick two blue beads (one is the last bead of the third row, the other is the first of the fourth row) and take the needle back through the first of these two beads.

14. Pull the thread tight to draw the two beads together, then take the needle through the next bead on the previous row.

15. Pick up two beads and take the needle through the next bead of the previous row.

16. Pull the thread tight, then, referring to the pattern to determine the bead colour required, repeat step 15 to the end of the row.

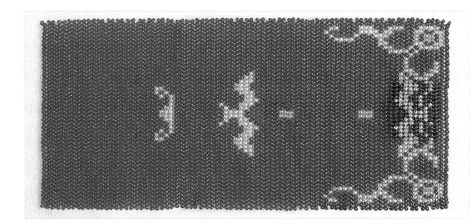

17. Working back and forth across the piece, and referring to the pattern to determine the bead colours, repeat steps 13–15 on all subsequent rows until all the herringbone work is finished. Weave the thread back into the piece and trim off the excess.

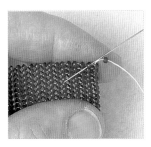

18. Weave in a new thread and exit it at the bottom, left-hand corner of the purse to start the picot edging. Pick up a blue bead and take the needle through the next bead along the side.

19. Take the thread up through the next bead on the side of the purse. Pick up another blue bead, take the needle through the next bead and pull the thread tight.

20. Repeat step 19 along the side of the front of the purse. Weave the thread into the work and trim off the excess. Use a new thread to work a picot edge along the opposite side of the back of the purse. Referring to page 29, work a gold picot edge round the three sides of the flap.

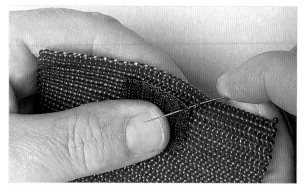

21. Sew a small strip of hook-and-eye fastener to the inside of the front flap and a mating strip to the outside of the front of the purse.

22. Complete the purse by sewing the sides together. Weave a thread through to exit at the top of the front of the purse, then sew down the side, working across through the picot bead and back through the next bead on the plain side. Weave the thread back into the beadwork and trim off the excess.

The finished purse

Amethyst bracelet

This bracelet, reproduced by kind permission of the owner, Gemma Cartwright, was worked in tubular herringbone stitch with size 11 seed beads and vintage feature beads. Beads that are more than twenty years old are commonly known as vintage beads and these feature beads were made in the 1950s. The clasp is a sterling silver T-bar and ring.

Summer dreams by Chrissy Bristow

A rope of beaded crochet. The spiral effect is created by using size 11 seed beads interspersed with 4mm crystals at each end, and size 8 beads and the same crystals in the centre section.

Morning glories by Chrissy Bristow

Bead crochet rope adorned with beaded flowers in herringbone stitch. The flowers are worked with size 11 deilca beads and have fresh-water pearls in their centres. The inspiration for the colour scheme came from an Elephant Hawk Moth that visited Chrissy's garden one summer.

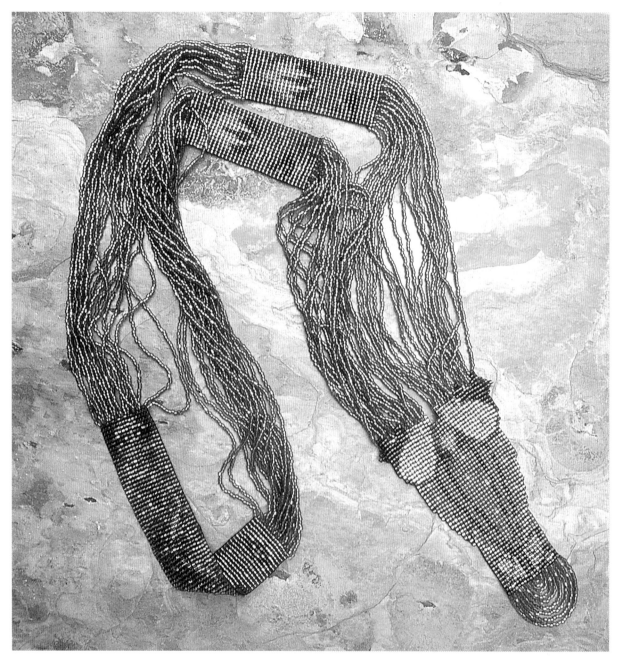

Nouveau tulips

This neck piece, worked with Delica beads, is based on the art nouveau style of the late 19th century. It was worked on a loom with the warp set for the widest part of the pendant panel The neck panel was worked as two equal length pieces, the ends of which were joined together when the piece was finally removed from the loom. When each panel was complete, the top of the warp was unwound, beads were strung on to each thread, then the warp was rewound on the loom. The bottom warp threads were strung with beads and woven back into the pendant panel to form the semicircular shape.

Opposite
Alice's collar

The rope for this collar was worked as one piece, then brick-stitch leaves were added to each end. The two large glass beads were encased with Peyote stitch then sewn on to the leaves. The adjustable slider was made in much the same way as shown on page 50.

Saraguro collars

This beautiful netted collar and the one opposite are typical of the work of the women of Saraguro village in Ecuador. No details of the patterns are written down – they are passed on by example and word of mouth. Both are worked with Czech beads and repeat netting.

Rombos by Zoila Chalan

Hojas by Zoila Chalan

Horizontal-net necklace

The string of gold beads for this necklace has a large bead and loop for the clasp. The rows of netting are worked horizontally, from one end of the string to the other, then back again.

The first row consists of eleven-bead loops (five main beads, one contrast bead and five main beads) connected to every tenth gold bead on the string.

The same size loops form the second row but these are connected to the contrast beads in the first row.

To ensure the correct shape, thirteen- bead loops are used for the third row and fifteen-bead loops for the fourth.

All the outer points of the net are decorated with three-bead picot edge.

Index

Sumatran sun hat

A modern piece of embroidered beadwork from Sumatra, made primarily for the tourist industry